Matthew Clark

Most Haunted Places in the United Kingdom

True Ghost Stories.

A Scary Journey in the Most Haunted Places in the United Kingdom

Table of Contents

Introduction

Haunted locales are a hot vacation destination for youngsters, adolescents, and grown-ups too. It is felt that over half of developed grown-ups have confidence in phantoms and the chance of a region being haunted. Britain is a zone that has dubious haunted action.

First is the High gate Cemetery. Situated in London, the High gate Cemetery is no common burial ground. In the event that you didn't have the foggiest idea about any better, you may figure that it was from the arrangement of a blood and gore movie. It is a main problem area for frequenting in Britain because of its ivy secured points, congested vegetation, and warped tombstones also adding to the air. Visits are accessible to permit vacationers to see this alongside the Gothic design here. Numerous individuals don't know that the acclaimed Karl Marx was covered here also.

Second is the Borley Rectory, which can be found in Essex. It was put on the map by Harry Price, who was an acclaimed eighteenth-century apparition tracker. The papers ran a tale about dubious action and a frequenting in the year 1929, which pulled him into the area. After Price researched, it was given the moniker of "The Most Haunted House in England" because of his discoveries. The structure itself didn't stand long a short time later and was decimated by a fire in the year 1939. Individuals actually have accounts of haunted encounters, and events and apparition trackers actually have it as one of their preferred spots to examine.

Another you can't miss is Pendle Hill, which is found in Lancashire. The whole region is called Pendle Witch Country,in which the slope overwhelms. This got its name from the occasions in 1612 of the "Witches of Pendle" preliminary where tenalleged witches were hanged at the Lancaster Castle. Numerous individuals accept that their spirits actually frequent the region.

Pendle Hill has been seen on Living TV's "Most Haunted."

Fourth, make certain to visit the Red Lion, Avebury, situated in Wiltshire. Numerous individuals clutch the possibility that an enormous number of Great Britain's bars are haunted. Some portion of the explanation is that bars, for the most part, are unfathomably old structures or the entertaining people imagine that apparitions may appreciate 16 ounces occasionally. The Red Lion Inn is 400 years of age and is viewed as one of the most haunted bars in all of Great Britain. That, as well as its area in the Avebury stone circle, Europe's most established, likewise expands its novel allure.

Last, yet absolutely not least, is the Glamis Castle in Scotland. It is more than 600 years of age, and the allure is promptly gotten when you see the pinnacles, sculptures, turrets, and towers. It has been named one of Scotland's most haunted manors, and the phantom most remarkable is the Monster of Glamis, who is supposed to be a twisted kid who was kept secured inside his room for an amazing term.

These are just a couple of the many haunted locations you will discover in all of England with its rich history.

There's something else entirely to England's noteworthy structures than meets the eye. While numerous currently welcome guests every day, some have their own paranormal guests that call them home.

As Halloween crawls nearer and nearer, join Alnwick Castle as we examine the most spooky spots in England and the UK all the more generally. With a significant number of the areas in our rundown open to people in general, perused these creepy stories and plan your visit today... if you dare!

Most Haunted is the well-known apparition chasing and paranormal show on UK Living TV. Facilitated by Yvette Fielding and her group of paranormal agents, including her better half Karl Beattie, this program's main arrangement was screened on Saturday, May 25th, 2002. Arrangement 1 explored seventeen haunted locations in the UK, including Chillingham Castle, Blackpool Pleasure Beach, Michel ham Priory and Derby Jail. The resulting scenes have highlighted a lot more also haunted places, which have made enthusiastic reviews.

The standard organization of the show is that the Most Haunted group travel around the UK and Ireland (and at times the United States, the most recent visit being in October 2007 to Winchester Mystery House, San Jose, CA) researching claimed paranormal 'hotspots' for 24 hours all at once.

Most Haunted by and large highlights the principle moderator (Yvette Fielding), a mystic medium and a parapsychologist. Basically, the last two make an even harmony among paranormal and logical clarifications for the different marvels. These are upheld by a portion of the creation team, who show up in the show and have some intelligence with different pieces of the examination while playing out their typical group job. Most of these on-screen team individuals likewise participate in séances, huge numbers of which have included the Ouija board's utilization.

Notwithstanding the ordinary week after week shows, there have been many Most Haunted Live shows. As a rule, these are around three hours long and run for a sum of three evenings. After every one of these live shows, watchers are allowed the chance to telephone into the show and remark on any paranormal movement they may have spotted on the different webcams the group has set up in each haunted area.

Most of the vigils highlighted in every scene include the utilization of night vision cameras, giving every area a genuine creepy climate. The photographic style of the arrangement has changed significantly since arrangement 1. Many expound shots were set up with an almost 'dramatic' style in the principal arrangement, with lit-up windows and dry ice. Locations were frequently enlightened outside in the evening, with blue and green hues. From arrangements 1 - 3, there was broad utilization of the Steadicam, which gave coasting shots during Yvette's spooky stories or general perspectives. In arrangement 8, the group presented a camera crane or 'Jib' framework for expounding airborne shots of both Yvette and the locations. Most of the photography in Most Haunted spotlights on 'general perspectives on's an area and its environmental factors. Most Haunted is shot with both transmission Sony DV cams and Sony PC120 mini DV cameras with night vision office.

The show has likewise highlighted visitor mediums. So far, these have been Derek Acorah, Ian Lawman, Ian Shillito, Gordon Smith, Uri Geller and Kevin Wade. A few scenes have additionally included at any rate one VIP. So far, famous people have included Vic Reeves, Nancy Sorrell, Gaby Roslin, Scott Mills, Mark Chapman, Simon Gregson, Sue Cleaver, Carol Thatcher, Paul O'Grady and Lee Ryan.

Most Haunted has delighted in an ever-expanding flood in fame; there have been numerous DVDs delivered of every arrangement, subtleties of which can be found beneath this article. Notwithstanding DVDs of the typical Most Haunted arrangement, DVDs have also been made of the Most Haunted Live shows.

Notwithstanding the DVDs, there have likewise been a few books delivered identifying with Most Haunted, to be specific Most Haunted and Ghost Hunters by Yvette Fielding and Ciaran O'Keefe.

The most ongoing live endeavor of Most Haunted was a seven-night examination at an old deserted mental asylum in Denbigh, North Wales. The Webmaster of the True Ghost Stories webpage shows up on the primary evening of this show.

The UK's Most Haunted Accommodations

Europe is saturated with history, and where there is history, there makes certain to be a phantom or two. That may be stressing for certain individuals; however, if you are a devotee of apparition stories, with a profound enthusiasm for the paranormal, and are arranging a visit through the UK, what could be in a way that is better than to book a night's stay in a haunted château, lodging, inn, or even a phantom ridden overnight boardinghouse. Peruse on for subtleties of a portion of the UK's most haunted accommodations.

At the point when a structure has a set of experiences returning for the best piece of 1000 years, it isn't unexpected to discover phantoms have supposedly been seen there. Amberley Castle in Sussex was established in the 12th-century, and its fortresses included the late 14th-century. Initially, the home of the Bishops of Chichester, Amberley, is presently a lavish lodging. In any case, there is one room at

Amberley where guests have been known to detect a paranormal presence. It is said that quite a while in the past, a working young lady at the palace fell pregnant subsequent to dawdling with a deviant religious administrator. Such was her disgrace and disrespect that she executed herself by jumping from the bastions adjoining the room thought to be haunted.

Arranged in Cumbria in the north of England, not a long way from the outskirt with Scotland, Dalston Hall is a lodging, previously a masterful habitation going back to the 15th-century. The inn has been highlighted on a few British TV shows examining apparitions and extraordinary occasions. In 2004 Dalston Hall was the subject of an element on "England's Most Haunted."A short time later, the moderator of the show revealed that it was the most alarming site the show had ever visited.

On the off chance that you travel around 100 miles northeast from London, you will go to the town of

Walberswick on the Suffolk coast. Convenience is accessible at the agreeable Anchor Inn, which notwithstanding its magnificent food and drink offers guests the chance, or danger, of encountering an apparition. On the off chance that that isn't sufficient to entice you, the close by St. Andrew's Church, a mostly demolished 15th-century building, is additionally accepted to be haunted. No less an individual than the notable creator George Orwell professed to have seen the phantom of an obscure man in the churchyard during the 1930s, and there have been other later sightings.

In Wales, in the Brecon Beacons (one of Britain's picturesque National Parks), is Craig-y-Nos Castle. This sentimental 19th-century house, when the home of a celebrated show vocalist, has been changed over into a very much designated nation lodging. In any case, just as its splendid offices for visitors, the lodging has made something for a name for itself by a method of appearances on TV shows researching haunting and unexplained occasions. For a period, the château was utilized as a clinic for terrible individuals, including numerous small kids experiencing progressed tuberculosis. It is believed that huge numbers of sightings of phantoms and different secretive sounds and occasions are associated with this.

These are only not many of the UK's most haunted accommodations. There are a lot more such foundations all over Britain, all "gloating" their own apparitions and phantoms. With so numerous to look over, there's not a phantom of a possibility you won't discover one to suit.

Haunted Hotels in England

Haunted houses are highly successful tourist destinations, but enchanted hotels have even greater exposure because more people have lived in them for a period of time, leading to more interesting stories and experiences for visitors.

One of the most visited enchanted hotels in all of England is the old Ram Inn, built in 1145. Attractions are ideal for ghosts with bare walls, dull areas, smells of moisture and old crispy floors. The current owner, John Humphreys, saved it from destruction in 1968, when he bought it for 2,600 pounds. Many TV and radio presenters visited this place, along with paranormal scientists who brought their technical equipment to capture strange activities. Strange smells, knocking from closed doors and puddles that appear casually, This Is What John often treats. Many people also think that a ghost named Elizabeth lives there, after being buried under the bar.

Another hotel famous for its ghosts is Dalston Hall in Cumbria. Lady Jane is often seen above the men's room in Tudor clothes. It was built in the 15th-century.Currently, it is a popular tourist place where people can see the Orange and red sandstone. Many people say they saw the Victorian ghost handyman when they came home until today at night.

While in England, do not miss the Elizabethan Talbot Hotel. Here is an oak staircase and other objects that have been transported from the ancient ruins of the Foveringei Castle. The spirit probably came from Mary, the Scottish queen, who went down the famous stairs until her execution.

Another famous haunted hotel that you should definitely visit or explore is The Highwayman Inn in Devon. It was originally founded in the XIII century. It was purchased in 1959, and owner John Jones repainted the interior to present a very marine theme. The gate of the ship Diana was used, and the sailors apparently died on that ship before finding their home in the hotel. The ship was trapped in the ice, and many sailors died without food and water. These sailors did not know another life, so they refused to leave the door. Their souls are stored in it at the hotel.

Last but not least, you should be intrigued by the Weston Manor Hotel in Oxford shire. It was a monastery in the 11th-century. The ghost that lives there is Maude's sister. He often visited the monks there, often gave them things or just stroked. She knew nothing else, and one night she was caught with a monk in a cell. She was accused of alienating the monk from his life path. He was burned at the stake right in front of the monastery, and the reverend received only a severe rebuke indicating a gender divergence. He visits the hotel's four-poster bed but does not want to hurt anyone.

Haunted Houses in England

Britain has numerous haunted locations, yet haunted houses appear to draw the most consideration and fascination, presumably on the grounds that we as a whole live in houses too and frequenting are both charming and terrifying too.

One of the most haunted houses in England is the Athelhampton Hall. It was initially suspected to be haunted in the 16th-century in Puddletown, Dorset. The house itself was first worked during the 15th-century by the Martyn family. Their family peak was enlivened by a pet monkey the family had, as told by their girl. The peak was a chimp sitting on a tree stump. Evidently, the girl secured herself a room and ended it all, and the monkey followed. It starved itself to death in there, and scratching is supposed to be heard.

Another haunted area is the Burton Agnes Hall. It is situated in Bridlington, East Yorkshire and was worked by Sir Henry Griffith, who administered from 1598-1610. The legend depends on his most youthful little girl Anne who had a wish that her skull ought to never be eliminated from the house. Anne was hit in a club by a homeless person who needed her ring, which eventually prompted her demise. Her body was covered, and slamming and smashing would not stop in the house. It was terrible to the point that her body was uncovered, and her skull was set in the house. Since the first event, two individuals have attempted to eliminate the skull; they were hopeless, so they at long last set it back. Nobody truly knows where it is in the house, and she says any individual who comprehends what is beneficial for them will disregard it.

A third haunted house is the Clandon House in West Clandon, Surrey and goes back to 1730. The first gardens from 1770 continue as before as they were. Giacomo Leoni was building the home for Lord Onslow and his better half. Sadly, his significant other passed on while it was being developed, and she is said to visit every now and then wearing a cream silk dress even though not mean in the soul.

Another prominent area in England is the Ightham Mote. It was implicit in 1340, and the frequenting started during the 17th-century. Dorothy Selb was said to have been bolted inside a room because the Gunpowder plot was found, and she got accused, although she cautioned Lord Monteagle not to go to parliament. A chill can be felt noticeable all around the pinnacles in view of this frequenting.

Moreton Corbet in Shropshire was inherent in 1606; however, Robert Corbet, who requested it fabricated, kicked the bucket before it was done, and his sibling Vincent took it over. Them two were Anti-Puritan despite the fact that Vincent was known for not detaining or mistreating them. He became friends with Paul Holymyard and afterward tossed him out to the forested areas and anticipated that he should fight for himself. Paul felt that he got him back by reviling the pathetic house with his soul once he got back to it after he kicked the bucket.

St. Briavels Castle

St. Briavels Castle is a magnet for Ghost pursuers, and rare types of people crossing their border searching for ghost experiences feel frustrated.

Surely, such is his notoriety for powerful events that he was named the most terrifying Castle in England.

The village was started in 1131 by Milo Fitz Walter, count of Hereford, to "control the invasions of the Welsh."

The dola of bread and cheese of St. Briavels

It was Milo who built one of the most experienced customs of the fortress, that of the Dole of bread and cheese of St Briavels. Every Sunday of Pentecost, locals wearing a middle-aged group gathers outside St. Briavels Castle to get cheddar bread and cheese thrown away by their dividers.

A pinnacle in the Enchanted Castle Of St. Briavels.

Castle of St. Briavels

Initially, a "recurring donation" was one that had paid a penny to the Earl of Hereford for the possibility of accumulating firewood from nearby wooden Hudnalls. Some accept that these pieces are saturated with supernatural properties (neighboring excavators, for example, thought that they could protect them from setbacks) and, in this way, protect them for good luck.

On Christmas Day 1143, Milo was killed by a street Bolt while chasing, and the castle of St. Briavels went to his son.

Over the next hundreds of years, the palace became the place of regulation for the Royal Forest of Dean and the room of the Royal Constable.

Governor John visits St. Briavels Castle

It was visited by some rulers, in particular by King John (1167-1216), who used it as a booth of persecution and is remembered today for the fact that the villa was called King John's bedroom in his honor. This room was used as a courthouse, and the writings on the stone of its gigantic fireplace are presumably the consequence of being hit with a blade every time someone was sentenced to death

Those who had anticipated the sentence and the individuals who had been convicted would be kept in the prison room arranged at the front door.

A strange atmosphere

Many of those who enter this room today comment on their unmistakably "peculiar" air, their feelings of unrest without uncertainty exacerbated by their dividers embellished with spray paint cut on them for quite some time in recent convicts. Robin Belcher. The day will come when you will answer why you swore against me, 1671, " explains a captivating model.

Since 1947, St Briavels Castle is one of the most interesting youth hostels in Britain, where seekers of provincial isolation can camp for a quiet night.

Meanwhile, people who come in search of more ethereal interests can undoubtedly anticipate the hustle and bustle of a beautiful evening.

The sad cry of a fantastic child

Lord John's bedroom hosts one of the palace's most constant apparitions, a hidden child whose pathetic cries alter as often as possible the dreams of those who sleep there.

The hanging room

In the hanging room, presumably, because it was the place where inmates who had been sentenced to death were led to anticipate their fate, willing Mystics often experience the alarming vibration of being grabbed by the throat.

The "oubliette" of the Castle

In the oubliette room, a carpet hides one of the castle's most chilling privileged perspectives. Throwing it back and lifting a hidden wooden entrance, you end up looking down into an evil Oubliette, a small prison, so-called by the French word Oubliette, meaning 'overlook,' where the sad hostages would be thrown and let themselves be transmitted.

Other ghosts of the Castle

Guests in the room felt that their clothes are pulled by hidden hands, while visitors who stay in bed here have been known to retreat unexpectedly at night, unable to bear their feeling that lasts longer.

Several spirits creeping into the villa incorporate a dark dog trotting through the rooms, a dim woman swimming along the Upper Room, and a knight in shining Shield appearing in the gardens.

The hallmark of History

History has certainly left its flaw in the weary dividers of time at St Briavels Castle, and the stories of his spooky adventures help illuminate boring corners of his fierce and memorable past. It is a place of crunchy wooden boards where for a long period of time, they coincide and converge sporadically with really disturbing results

St. Briavals Castle is regularly alluded to as the most spooky château in the UK. Today, the mansion is utilized as a young lodging; however, with significant paranormal action detailed levels, it may not be the ideal decision for getting a decent night's rest!

A portion of the unusual goings-on has been accounted for incorporate hearing the calls of an infant originating from King John's Bedroom, while different guests have felt their garments being pulled by concealed hands. Spooky figures spotted at the mansion incorporate a dark canine who meanders the rooms, a dim woman at the top hallway and a knight strolling the château's grounds.

In general, guests have revealed a staggering sentiment of persecution, as though something supernatural is available. Truth be told, a few visitors have supposedly left halfway through their stay as a result of it.

Chillingham Castle

Chillingham Castle, Northumberland, UK, is considered the most haunted castle in the UK and not by chance, as the castle houses dark dungeons and creepy torture chambers. This ancient fortress dates back to 1246 when the Lords of Count Gray built this wonderful building and where the ancestors of Count Gray lived for centuries.

The castle is currently home to Sir Humphrey Wakefield Bt.. his wife Lady Wakefield and her family. The family claims that this is the most visited castle because of the multitude of ghosts that often roam their home.

The most obvious spectral aspect is "Blue Boy" (or "Shining Boy"), which is said to chase the Pink Room of the castle. Many guests, occupying the room, heard the terrible groans, soon followed by a halo of blue light that appeared above their bed.

Although this disturbing detail ended when a disturbing discovery during the repair revealed the bones of a boy and a man who had been walled inside the wall, it was clear that no one should have heard his miserable cries for help since the wall was built 10 feet thick.

It wasn't the end of the infestations at Chillingham Castle. Homeowners also witnessed much more sinister energy wandering the corridors, the scary ghost of once the evil torturer John Sage.

John Sage is the Ghost of an Evil past

When the night comes around Chillingham Castle, one of the scariest sounds you sometimes hear is "something" that slowly drags your foot as you wander through the corridors. It is believed that the spirit of former lieutenant John Sage who earned the nickname "dragfoot" when, in life, his leg was wounded by a spear during his last battle in the current wars with its neighbors in Scotland.

After the injury, he was in desperate need of work and was proud to have received the title of tormentor of Chillingham Castle from Castle owner Edward Longshanks (1200 A.D.). The Sage was a human monster, and his terrible work would bring him enormous satisfaction for the next three years, where he would continue to torment at least 50 of his Scottish enemies a week.

Sage rejoiced when the Scots were captured and thrown into the dungeons of the castle. These poor souls would like to die on the battlefield, as Sage was famous for the most horrible tortures in history. The torture device has become known as one of the most terrible "cell". This apparatus will capture his victim and then be placed on a burning fire to fry the prisoner for hours while Sage SAT studies his enemy-writhing and screaming for his death.

Sage's insatiable thirst for torture would have led to his fall when his mistress Elizabeth Charlton once visited him. During their sexual relationship, Sage decided to put Elizabeth on one of her other torture devices: the shelf. Sage then started choking her sexual pleasure but went too far and accidentally killed her.

Elizabeth's father (on the Borderline Reiver, clan leader and Outlaws), after learning of his daughter's death, warned Longshanks, now almost penniless, if he had not been killed, the Sage will join an allied attack with the Scots against the castle.

Longshanks' reduced resources due to the war and the fact that the border guards were a powerful force gave him more choice than putting Sage to death. He was hanged in the castle at The 'Devil's Mile'(aka Devil's Walk) in front of a crowd of mocking spectators.

As the Sage's body continued to contract with life, the crowd surrounded him, cutting off pieces of his body, including his nose, toes and testicles. A rather "acute" fate, some might say, for the fact that the greatest admiration was the vision of an evil end.

"Chillingham Castle" by Andrew Stawarz is authorized for use under CC BY-ND 2.0.

Visit Chillingham Castle, and you could well get chills, as the manor brags some of the most significant paranormal movement levels in the nation.

Numerous phantoms and devils have been located at the stronghold, with some getting famous in any event. The White Pantry Ghost is a delicate white figure seen around The Inner Pantry. Some time ago, the storeroom used to store silver, with a footman utilized to rest in the room and keep watch. One night, he was visited by a woman in white who beseeched him for water. Obliging reasoning the lady was a château visitor, the man immediately understood the storeroom was bolted, and nobody could have entered!

Other paranormal movement incorporates the inclination that somebody is watching you in the chamber, just as the voices of two men in the house of prayer that dubiously stop when you approach where it's coming from.

Various Attractions when visiting Haunted Chillingham Castel

If you want to visit any kind of haunted castles or lodging where paranormal movement happens, at that point, you may be intrigued to visit Chillingham Castle in England. Indeed, even the name recommends chills and excites! This manor is situated in Chillingham, which is on the north side of Northumberland and is encircled by grass, gardens and thick woods. You can likewise see the Chillingham Wild Cattle from the mansion grounds as an additional ox-like reward.

In England, Chillingham Castle was worked during the bygone eras and gave a military fortress as it was situated between two countries who were continually battling. The English armed force utilized the manor to enter Scotland and assault the Scottish armed force. With a rich history of fights and executions, the stronghold is known to be haunted and is exceptionally mainstream among a few TV and radio projects.

Haunted Castles - Blue Boy?

A portion of the shows that have examined or covered this heavenly area incorporate Holiday Showdown, Most Haunted, Scariest Places On Earth, Alan Robson's Nightowls, I'm Famous and Frightened!, and Ghost Hunters International.

Various spirits have been accounted for processing about the huge stronghold. The most celebrated is the "Blue Boy." He is regularly observed by sightseers and cries and groans in distress or maybe from fear directly around 12 PM. His groans appear to originate from a region close to an entry cut through a ten-foot divider. As the shouts blur, a hover of shining light can be seen encompassing a four banner bed. Woman Mary Berkeley is another normally seen apparition. She is generally located meandering around discouraged and carelessly. Many accept that she is on an interminable mission to discover her sister, Lady Mary. Others report hearing the stir of her dress and calm strides.

Another abhorrent fascination for this haunted excursion objective is the insidious dungeon of Chillingham Castle. A few torment instruments are still in plain view, including an extending rack, a bed of nails, a nailed barrel and a spiked seat (marked with a notice not to sit on it!), the Iron Maiden, thumb screws, leg irons, chains and marking irons.

Today, Chillingham Castle in England can be visited by the general society. The exquisite château also makes it self-accessible for lease for occasions like visits, private capacities, weddings and works, and self-providing food lofts. Numerous weddings have occurred at the Medieval and Elizabethan staterooms. The patio has South yard wellsprings and with the Italian nursery makes it the best spot to have a get-together.

There are formal nurseries and yards which incorporate a shrubbery garden having cut fences. Throughout the spring and summer season, their gardens are a sight to appreciate. Those of you who like to go fishing at waterway Till, can get a fishing license for £10 every day from the castle. There is a seashore close by that gives you some wonderful view. At the point when you pick Chillingham Castle as your haunted excursion location, you get a lot of frightens and the lighter side of normal excellence as well!

Whitby Abbey

One of the numerous historical sites you can appreciate when visiting the fabulous Whitby territory, Yorkshire, is the excellent destruction of Whitby Abbey.

The remnants are arranged on a beachfront headland and look out over the town of Whitby beneath. The towns associated with the Abbey ruins by a precarious arrangement of steps wrapping up the slope's side, which is the conventional course and develops upon the headland before the noteworthy stone dividers.

The Abbey itself has experienced a few corrections from before. It began being a little area church worked in around 1090 AD. This congregation was then changed into the bigger Abbey around 1220 AD, undoubtedly because of the expansion in the priest populace. Yet, the more established church dividers can, in any case, today be found in places around the site.

When the choice to build another monastery on the site was taken in 1220 AD, apparently, the priests also chose to extraordinarily develop the congregation that existed on the site. The subsequent monastery was one of the most goal-oriented structures of the time, an excellent early Gothic design case.

Throughout the long term, the Abbey got one of the most extravagant in the nation up until its stature soon after 1220 AD; however, a lot of these riches dwindled throughout the long term following the reproduction because of broad development costs. These developments included incredible recolored glass windows, one of which portrayed William the Conqueror, and lovely stone carvings demonstrating the region's history alongside strict scenes. A significant part of the stonework actually endures. It's as yet conceivable to get a vibe of what the Abbey probably has been similar to at its stature. Added to this, the Abbey would have had a flawlessly painted ensemble and an amazing transept.

As we see it today, the Abbey is a shell of its previous wonder; the impression of its radiance is still there; however, this is chiefly a direct result of the disregard the structure endured in the seventeenth century. The top of the Abbey was deprived of its lead for cash, leaving it helpless against the components; in the long run, prompting the breakdown of both the pinnacle and the nave and leaving the Abbey in the condition it tends to be found in today.

The site is an incredible open door for anybody remaining in one of the numerous Whitby Hotels in the region to enjoy the territory's history.

Whitby might be most popular as the motivation for Bram Stoker's Dracula; however, there is all the more connecting this Northern fishing town to the paranormal than just vampires. Truth be told, Whitby is evidently home to no under 12 vile creatures.

As per prevalent thinking, you'll face one of two destinies on the off chance that you investigate the well at Whitby Abbey at 12 PM. Those with an unadulterated heart will see the substance of St. Hilda, while those without are accepted to be cleared away by the villain.

Additionally, located in the territory is a spooky funeral car complete with headless ponies and driver, which has been found before St Mary's Church before dashing along the cliff tops and into the ocean.

Take a visit to the notable Whitby Abbey

Whitby Abbey overwhelms the town of Whitby from the east precipice. It's an incredible token of the early intensity of the congregation, an extraordinary bit of design.

Climb the 199 stages to the monastery to appreciate perspectives on the untainted excellence of Whitby Harbor, the EskValley and the great Yorkshire coastline. The Abbey ruins themselves are an extraordinary motivation to numerous individuals, even Bram Stoker, who based aspect of his notable novel "Dracula" on the motivation from Whitby Abbey.

In the event that that sounds minimal bristly startling, you could generally have a walk around one of the awesome nurseries encompassing Whitby Abbey, also one of the UK's best Youth Hostels nearby to the Abbey, absolutely Whitby Abbey is one of the most adored UK attractions.

Whitby Museum is loaded with history

The Museum is an autonomous Museum with numerous incredible presentations. Whitby Museum contains a wide variety of presentations that will keep the two Adults and Children intrigued. In some cases, the gallery is one of the most far-reaching in Yorkshire.

Among the assortments are old fossils, stream, Capt. James Cook and William Scoresby (whaling and logical instruments) display many model boats, common history, archaic exploration, former events, ensembles, toys and dolls, ethnography, samplers, pottery, militaria, coins and decorations, just as the renowned 'Hand of Glory' and substantially more.

Tower of London

With a set of experiences characterized by detainment and passing, you'd expect a couple of phantoms and fiends sneaking around the Tower of London. There have been numerous reports of paranormal activity in the pinnacle throughout the long term, with some, in any event, professing to see ghosts of previous rulers strolling the grounds.

Guests have revealed seeing the apparitions of two youthful rulers — accepted to be Edward and Richard, who strangely vanished in around 1483. The young men are frequently located in the White Tower.

Another regal soul said to visit the pinnacle is the headless apparition of Anne Boleyn, who was guillotined at the pinnacle in 1536. Her phantom has been seen in numerous territories of the pinnacle both all around, including the Chapel of St Peter, where she was covered.

Edinburgh's South Bridge Vaults

Haunted Places in British cities are many, but Hamburg offers the most skeptical people a real chance to delve into the dark side of this past city.

Last year, the most haunted team came to Edinburgh Street for one of their live polls. For those of you who are unfamiliar, this is a show found on Living TV in which a group of paranormal researchers nests around a place trying to get in touch with ghosts, cue screams and Green Night Vision TV. The show of the first night visited the famous Times of Edinburgh, a maze of rooms discovered in the mid-1980s under Edinburgh's South Bridge. Since the public had access to the room, special warning tales have been reported on numerous occasions.

In the vaults, the team reported feelings of illness and heard constantly calling during investigations, with some cast members even collapsing. On the second night of the investigation, the cast members were actually cut in the legs during live television!! This is all cause for debate, but the place is very disturbing and worth a visit. When these times were really busy, it is said that the notorious Body Snatchers Burke and Hare may have used the times to get the bodies that were then sold to the nearby hospital.

Edinburgh is a place worth visiting at any time, and the number of hotels in Edinburgh means that all budgets are met. But Edinburgh and its past space are definitely worth investigating, and times are one of the most intriguing places to investigate.

"Edinburgh Vaults" by Nelo Hotsuma is authorized under CC BY 2.0.

For the following passage in our rundown of the most spooky spots in the UK, we travel to Scotland for Edinburgh's South Bridge Vaults, found profound underground.

While a few structures become frequented after some time, it's generally accepted that the South Bridge

Vaults were reviled from the off. In 1788, the city's most seasoned inhabitant was making the initial authority crossing into the vaults, yet she kicked the bucket before its finishing. Her casket was the first to cross the extension, driving numerous occupants to accept the scaffold was reviled.

With the vaults dismissed by organizations and taken up as habitation by probably the most urgent in the public eye, it's accounted for that Burke and Hare would utilize the vaults to discover bodies.

Numerous phantoms are said to frequent the vaults today, with guests revealing seeing spooky nebulous visions and some, in any event, enduring scratches and wounds. One radio chronicle from 2003 made in the vaults was most frightfully unusable because of a Gaelic voice allegedly cautioning the moderators to "disappear!"

Historical Attractions in Edinburgh Will Leave You fascinated and Freaked-out!

Edinburgh's historical attractions are copious, yet the beautiful history of our capital city can be seen, felt and found out about on pretty much every traffic intersection.

Try not to be tricked by the peacefulness; Edinburgh is a city with an energetic and brutal history. It was once home to fierce killers, grave burglars and man-eaters who have left local people with in excess of a small bunch of stories that will make your blood run cold— find out about it at the Edinburgh Dungeon!

'Auld Reekie' (or 'Old Smoky,' Edinburgh's epithet because of the famously helpless air quality before) is additionally a city of essayists, designers and sovereignty.

Widely acclaimed creators Sir Walter Scott and Sir Arthur Conan Doyle were both conceived in

Edinburgh, as was Alexander Graham Bell, the designer of the phone.

For history buffs, the main stop in Edinburgh ought to consistently be Edinburgh Castle. Our town's crown gem has consistently been and consistently will be the most significant of the apparent multitude of historical attractions in Edinburgh.

Having assumed a part in the key sections of Scottish history, for example, the Wars of Independence and the Jacobite uprising, a visit to Edinburgh Castle is basically a visit through Scottish history itself.

Slanting downhill from Edinburgh Castle to Holyrood Palace, the Royal Mile or High Street is the foundation of Edinburgh's Old Town and the most celebrated road in Scotland. It is additionally your place of a plunge into Edinburgh's dim past on one of our acclaimed phantom visits.

At the lower part of the Royal Mile, you will locate the cutting edge tent-like structure which houses Our

Dynamic Earth. This astonishing intelligent exhibition hall will fill your boots with the history of our planet if Edinburgh's vivid history isn't sufficient for you!

A short stroll from the Royal Mile down George IV Bridge will take you to the National Museum of Scotland, where you can become familiar with Scotland's history and its kin. Historical attractions in Edinburgh show up everywhere.

The mile-long High Street has assumed a focal part in the history of Edinburgh since the 12th-century. When the area of an outdoors exchanging market, the Royal Mile got home to a huge number of individuals when wood structures were set up, the holes between these structures were and still are alluded to as 'closes.' On your visit to the Royal Mile, make certain to investigate the many rear entryways which branch off the central avenue.

After the decimation of the archaic municipality in 1544 by the English, stone lodging was raised and the

Royal Mile bit by bit turned out to be increasingly more packed. By the mid-seventeenth century, around 70,000 individuals considered the Royal Mile their home.

Modernization of the road occurred during the 19th-century and started to assume the presence of the Royal Mile we see today—as you stroll down this road, attempt to envision what life resembled in those days, the foulness, the earth and ailment. It is hard to locate a more particular road anyplace on the planet. Of the apparent multitude of historical attractions in Edinburgh, it is surely the most barometrical.

The Old Town of Edinburgh

Viably, the part of the downtown area toward the south of Princes Street Gardens and Edinburgh Castle is the Old Town. This piece of Edinburgh, alongside the New Town, is a UNESCO world legacy site.

Being arranged on the slants of the volcanic Castle Rock, the Old Town is spread out on various levels. Importance steep roads, tight back streets and little extensions are the standard. As I would see it, this makes the Old Town a great area to investigate and get lost!

In the previous thirty years, underground vaults have been found at once for capacity and as living quarters for generally poor merchants. Likewise, chronic executioners Burke and Hare scoured the vaults for expected casualties and put away bodies there!

Edinburgh's acclaimed phantom visits will give you admittance to certain areas of the vaults and to underground roads like Mary King's Close, which were allegedly stopped during the 17ᵗʰ-century to contain the spread of the bubonic plague. Historical attractions in Edinburgh don't come more alarming than that!

These days, the Old Town, where 80,000 individuals lived in the eighteenth century, is incredibly mainstream among local people and travelers hoping to find out around ten centuries of history and invest energy in a portion of the endless bars, bars and clubs which line pretty much every city intersection.

Territories of the Old Town like the Cow gate and the Grass market, which was a position of execution in times passed by, are currently celebrating hotspots. It is an uncommon inclination unwinding with your companions in conventional bars and current home bases encompassed by many long stretches of history.

Grey friars Bobby

The account of Grey friars Bobby is one that has contacted the hearts of endless individuals around the globe.

Bobby was a Skye Terrier who had a place with Mr. John Gray, a night guardian for the Edinburgh City Police. Subsequent to going through two years forever by his proprietor's side, Bobby was left to fight for himself when Gray tragically kicked the bucket of tuberculosis in the winter of 1858.

The little Terrier went through the most recent fourteen years of his life, guarding John Gray's grave in Grey friars Kirkyard in Edinburgh's Old Town. Grey friars Bobby passed on in 1872 and was covered close to the door of Grey friars Kirkyard just a couple of meters from his proprietor's grave.

This long-term showcase of steadfastness and dedication contacted the nearby residents. Lady Burdett-Coutts had a little sculpture of Bobby set up at the intersection of George IV Bridge and Candle maker Row a year after his passing. This sculpture has gotten one of the most mainstream and noteworthy historical attractions in Edinburgh.

This story has produced various books and movies, and Bobby's sculpture and the grave have gotten mainstream with sightseers and local people wishing to offer their appreciation to the dedicated animal.

Such is the significance of Bobby's heart-delivering story to the individuals of Edinburgh; it is as much an aspect of Edinburgh's history as some other key figure or occasion.

The Edinburgh Dungeon

All things considered, the Edinburgh Dungeon isn't for the cowardly! Truth be told, it is certainly the creepiest, most terrifying yet seemingly the most-engaging of the apparent multitude of historical attractions in Edinburgh.

The dungeon is situated in Market Street, close to Waverley Train Station, a stones toss from Princes Street and will ship you back into Edinburgh and Scotland's dim and out hazardous past! Despite the fact that most nations have a vile, suspect history, Scotland truly does stand apart from the rest with regards to kill, inbreeding, barbarianism, burglary, sickness and wicked war—have I put you off yet?

For reasons unknown, we Scots really prefer to discuss our dim past as though it's something to be pleased of as an outcome; we have the Edinburgh Dungeon—a fascination stuffed with shows, enhancements, hair-raising rides and trepidations which give you a very genuine knowledge into our brutal past!

You'll get some answers concerning age-old torment strategies, insensitive lawbreakers, the destiny of Scottish nationalist William Wallace and the ruthless violations of a portion of Edinburgh's most infamous killers, for example, Burke and Hare and Sawney Bean's family.

In the event that you actually have your stomach within proper limits after all that, give the scandalous Extremis ride a go. I'll let you get some answers concerning that one yourself! Opening occasions shift consistently, yet the Edinburgh Dungeon's opening times are commonly longer throughout the mid-year months and at the ends of the week.

It will be ideal if you be cautioned in any case! On the off chance that I routinely approach free inside condition at the Edinburgh Dungeon, small kids could likewise discover this fascination upsetting. It will be ideal if you utilize your own discretion, oh, and don't attempt any of what you see at home!

The Edinburgh Museum of Childhood

What makes this historical center so special is the reality it was the absolute first of its sort on the planet in 1955. No other gallery had some expertise in the history of adolescence before the Edinburgh Museum of Childhood opened its entryways.

The gallery not just glances at the manner in which kids were raised and instructed in Scotland yet also shows toys and games from around the world to give guests a global point of view on youth.

Among the galleries, various mixed media shows are the 1930s study hall and the 1950s road games display where guests can see how kids were instructed and how they engaged themselves in the long term since passed.

One of the most famous historical attractions in Edinburgh among small kids, families and youth on a fundamental level grown-ups, the Museum of Childhood has endless youngsters' toys, games and articles from over a significant time in plain view and numerous sound accounts of kids singing and playing as you stroll through the gallery.

Confirmation is free, so it's an incredible method to keep youngsters (and yourself!) engaged without putt.

Dark Swan Hotel, York

In view of its status as a notable city, York is home to many frequented areas, not exactly The Swan Hotel, which goes back to the 15th-century.

There have been numerous otherworldly goings-on at the inn throughout the long term, to where the lodging currently pulls in customary phantom trackers keeping watch for paranormal movement. As indicated by reports, the apparition of a man wearing a bowler cap is frequently spotted at the bar, while the figure of a young lady in a white dress has been seen gazing into the chimney.

Maybe the most abnormal of everything is the reports of two legs — autonomous of a body — spotted strolling around the lodging.

Pendle Hill, Lancashire

Pendle Hill in Lancashire can be viewed as one of England's most spooky spots on account of its association with the Lancashire witch preliminaries.

The area was home to twelve charged witches in the 17th-century, who were accepted to have killed ten individuals. While one kicked the bucket during the preliminary, 10 of the witches were hung while one was seen not as blameworthy.

Today, the witches are said to frequent the structures and towns of Pendle Hill. Guests to the apparition visits that occur are said to feel outrage, with some in any event, feeling like they were choked by spooky hands.

Hampton Court Palace

An imperial apparition is said to frequent Hampton Court Palace. Henry VIII's significant other, Catherine Howard, is accepted to frequent a particular segment of the palace. Legend has it that when Howard was captured at the castle, she got away from the watchmen and ran along the passageway to the Chapel Royal.

Accepting the King to be in supplication, Catherine shouted for kindness. She was later executed at the Tower of London. Guests to the royal residence have detailed odd sensations when strolling the hall, accepted to be the presence of Catherine's phantom.

The royal residence is additionally supposedly home to the phantom of Sybil Penn, a previous worker who passed on of little pox subsequent to nursing Elizabeth I when she experienced the illness. Spooky action started in 1829 when her burial place was moved, with guests revealing hearing the hum of a turning wheel — which was later found in a little fixed chamber.

In June 2005, I visited the building with Terry, who meets a gamekeeper from Hampton Court, Les. Terry and they are old friends and had worked for them at Hampton Court Palace since they were 16 years old. Now he is fifty, and Queen Elizabeth II was honored in September for his services to the crown. And he was able to tell us things about the palace that most of the public does not necessarily know. He also told us some of his personal experiences during his time at Hampton Court Place, and they were very interesting!

Today, the only Hampton Court Palace residents are those who work there, like Les and his wife. At one time, it was used by the inhabitants of "grace and kindness", that is, people who were granted accommodation without rent " by the grace and kindness of the ruler. These were usually people or their employees who gave great service to the crown or the country. In Hampton Court Palace today, there are still some inhabitants of "grace and kindness."

Our first stop was the kitchen. They are huge, and they had to be because Henry's entourage of 1300 courtiers traveled everywhere with him. Imagine feeding and housing this number of people when appliances such as dishwashers, microwave ovens and dryers were even more than an unrealizable dream of electricity. In the kitchens, there were several cooks at work. He prepared a typical meal from the Tudor period of Henry exactly as he would have prepared in the years of his reign-1509-1547.

This meant manually cutting meat, manually grinding spices and herbs, collecting mushrooms from the forest and cooking on a wooden fire. A large piece of meat was baking on a skewer turned by two teenagers, and the juice from the meat dripped into a pan full of potatoes cooked on coals. The second cook prepares the same dish with products purchased at the local Tesco supermarket branch so that everything has already been sliced, crushed and marinated and cooked in the microwave or on the gas stove! At the end of our tour, we returned to the kitchen to see if there really was any variation of flavors, hoping that we could offer you some flavor. It seems they both knew each other very similar, but both chefs said the main difference was the taste of traditionally cooked Tudor food that lasted longer than modern food. Our mouths were watering as we watched rare slices of roast beef and Yorkshire pudding with tasty, crispy roast potatoes laid out on a beautiful ceramic plate. Unfortunately, despite our very obvious hunger, we were not offered any!

There is a beautiful chapel on site, and wedding ceremonies are still held there to this day. It has a blue ceiling decorated with Golden Stars and decorative ceramic figures painted in gold. The dark wood paneling is beautifully carved and gives the chapel nobility. The King had his entrance to the chapel, and the ceiling and walls are covered with images of cherubs and nymphs floating around the beautiful blue sky along with water, lush green flora and live fauna and deer. Unfortunately, the Chapel, The King and Queen apartments, The Grand Hall and some associated rooms are all that is left of Henry VIII. William III. and Mary II commissioned Sir Christopher Wren to rebuild Hampton Court Palace at the end of the 17th-century. It's a pity because Tudor architecture is magnificent, rich and very royal. The rest of the court is impressive but lacks the absolute "royal" Henry's cameras demonstrate so vividly.

The rooms are filled with huge tapestries and paintings of various courtiers and hunting scenes. Part of the Queen's famous art collection is stored in the palace, but it is not exhibited to the public. All the rooms of the palace are huge, and there are fireplaces in almost all. There are more than 1, 000 fireplaces throughout the building, and the fireplace above the Tudor sections have different brick structures.

Being an old building, one would expect that residents would include a ghost or two, and we were not disappointed. The fifth wife of Henry VIII., Catherine

Howard, was imprisoned in the rooms of her palace. She was married to Henry for only 15 months, and he was sentenced to death for adultery. Before she was taken to the Tower of London to be executed, she tells the story that she escaped from her rooms and ran to the chapel's door where the King was attending a religious service. She wanted to beg for her life, but when she got to the door, the guards grabbed her and dragged her screaming into their rooms. People in the palace claim that the spirit still runs screaming along the gallery that leads to the chapel's door.

There are other ghosts that people have seen—they claim that they have not seen anyone, but there are employees who have heard or seen "something." I went into a small room believed to be Henry's most famous wife, Anne Boleyn before they took her to meet their executioner. It is located next to Henry's Great Hall, and it is said that it was deliberately placed there. Anne, alone and trapped in her small room, could hear Henry and his court eating and eating and rising to all sorts of malice as she sat alone and contemplated her fate.

The palace covers six acres, and the gardens occupy another 60 acres. The palace is located on 600 acres and is home to a herd of 300 deer, various ducks and some very elegant swans. We went for a carriage ride along one of the watercourses and visited the greenhouses. The gardens are now cared for by 30 gardeners; when the palace was used by the Royal, the number of gardeners exceeded 150! We visit Fountain Court and clock Court, which is famous for the huge 24-hour clock located under the bell tower. Built in 1540 is a water clock, not only showing the right time but also the date and tide! There are many gardens, each of which is unique and well maintained.

Ghost image captured by CCTV at Hampton Court

Hampton Court Palace is home to the oldest known Vine in the world. Planted in 1768, it still produces grapes (unfortunately, no green varieties without seeds), and when we visited, there were more than 1000 grapes in all. Jill is the official administrator; visitors can watch the video through the glass window, but thanks to our guides, we were able to enter the glasshouse that protects the see a group of about 30 people, looked at us through the glass; I think it is the experience of the fish tank, which we've heard a lot. Hampton Court maze is Britain's most famous maze, and I hate to admit we were lost twice! There were many other people who tried to solve the maze puzzle, and they got lost like us! In the sheep maze "baaaing" there are some sound effects, shots and voices of men and women telling us: "Oh, dear, lost again "or" I turned wrong!"certainly added to the experience.

On a tour of the palace, I saw maybe 25 percent of the whole place. Amazing, isn't it that so many rooms are empty and abused today when they were once full of people who lived their lives to the fullest? We've seen some rooms empty, and most of them are bigger than a modern bed! What a sad loss of space. What a wonderful story!

Felbrigg Hall

Next up on our summary of frequented places in the UK is Felbrigg Hall in Norfolk. Legend has it that the lobby is spooky by book-darling and previous inhabitant William Windham III.

In 1809, a fire broke out in Windham's companion's library. As an admirer of books, he could not see the books die in the fire, so he took a chance with his life to rescue a portion of the releases. Continuing horrendous wounds, Windham passed on half a month later.

The apparition of Windham has been seen in the library at Felbrigg on numerous events, either at the table or situated in a seat. Many accept he has gotten back to the library to wrap up his assortment, while a few reports recommend the phantom possibly shows up when certain books are open.

A 17th-century house with a nursery and park. The recreation center has woods and a lakeside walk. A-Ha isolates the recreation center from the nursery. The nursery has a wonderful block dovecote. The walled kitchen garden presently contains herbaceous plants and natural product trees prepared against the dividers. On a desolate plain, the home once had a place with William Wyndham, who begat the expression that the parks are 'the lungs of London.' Humphry Repton utilized his library when considering scene planting as a vocation, and a portion of his initial thoughts on improving areas was shaped while watching out on the desolate plain. The Copper Plate Magazine (1793-98) commented that 'The extraordinary magnificence of Felbrig Park comprises in the degree and magnificence of its woods, essentially of oak and beech of huge measurements. To these are yearly including new ranches, under the heading of Mr. Kent, creator of Hints to Gentlemen of Landed Property'.

Alnwick Castle

To wrap things up on our rundown is our one of a kind, Alnwick Castle. While it mightn't be the most spooky spot in England, there have been some abnormal goings-on throughout the long term, to be specific, from the Alnwick Vampire!

Legend has it that a man who served the master of Alnwick Castle associated his significant other with having an unsanctioned romance. Intending to get her in the demonstration, he climbed onto the top of their home and tumbled to his demise in the wake of breaking his neck.

Notwithstanding being covered, the man was spotted around the town! At the point when ailments spread, and animals started biting the dust, local people normally presumed the man. They uncovered his carcass to think that it's engorged with blood. When the body was discarded, the appearances and ailments strangely halted.

Right up 'til the present time, the man is known as the Alnwick Vampire. The name got from archaic recorder William of Newburgh, who utilized the term 'bloodsucker' to depict the man in his record of the story – the main recorded utilization of the word in England.

In case you're sufficiently bold, why not book your passes to our extraordinary occasion, Alnwick Castle After Dark: Below Stairs? Running all through October, it's the ideal get ready for Halloween, as we bring you into the dividers of Alnwick Castle to find the vile mysteries of this middle age manor.

Alnwick, which is located in the north-east of England, is located in the county of Northumberland. Although at Castle Alnwick, it has a very profitable tourist attraction,it does not depend solely on its economy.

Previously, Alnwick depended on agriculture and its administration to provide jobs for the city's residents. Agriculture was the original reason for the settlement, which began in 600 AD. The story of Alnwick, however, is actually the story of the castle, which became a setting for Percy's battles with the Scots. The Scottish assault Party effectively razed much of the city in 1424.

It was also the stopping point for the first major North Road between London and Edinburgh.

The population of Alnwick is currently 31,029. There has been a large increase in population over the past decade, mainly due to housing and commercial flourishing properties on the city's outskirts. This allowed both people to escape from the larger city of Newcastle and into smaller cities, where there is little hope of economic prosperity, to become part of Alnwick.

Country Life magazine in 2004 said in a review of Alnwick, "the most picturesque market town, "and declared "the best place to live in Britain."The great advantage of Alnwick has its position. Situated 32 miles south of Berwick-upon-Twee and the Scottish Borders, Newcastle lies within the commuter train belt.

Alnwick Castle is the second largest inhabited castle in the United Kingdom. The first is Windsor Castle. For six months a year, the castle is open to tourists, and the surrounding gardens are open all year round. Due to its many historical and original features, Alnwick Castle has been used for many filming locations and described as Hogwarts in Harry Potter films.

If you are planning a trip to Alnwick Castle, a gift awaits you. You are about to be thrown into a rich and ancient history that goes back to the great wars that disturbed the land in 1172 and 1174 when the infamous and voracious Scottish king (King William Lion) besieged the Kingdom and caused confusion for all the inhabitants of the area.

Fortunately, the great castle survived the conquest of King William, and now it is still here, alive and restored so that we can appreciate its greatness. The castle was built by Ivo de Vesci, who used wood and mortar for most of its construction. Although the Percy family had to make dramatic changes to restore the castle to a state that would stand the test of time, you can still see many views of the past construction in all its nooks and crannies. Like the castle's bloody past, even the Percy family was never far from the controversy. Thomas Percy was even beheaded by Queen Elizabeth no less, in 1572. In more recent times, Sir Hugh Smithson became the first Duke of Northumberland in 1766. He was mainly responsible for much of the restoration of the castle.

From 1755, its renovation is often appreciated by the use of Gothic architecture. The renovations were, in general, impressive, even in their time. Since then, architectural history students from nearby and distant universities still visit the castle to explore its unique blends of masonry and wood. It is really an act of craftsmanship when, compared to the technology of the time, the number of good people of the time was really able to achieve with so little and with little at their disposal. After his death, the second Duke of Northumberland actually served in the American War of independence. Even at this time, the Constable's tower was used as an armory for the army. And he fulfilled his purpose of alienating people like Napoleon Bonaparte. But the story continues, as the castle played a role in the lives of 6 other Dukes. And only after the sixth Duke of Northumberland began a major replenishment and restoration. In many ways, he is largely responsible for the castle as we know it today, and seeing the good craftsmanship of the time will certainly be a fun family experience.

Heathrow London

The period of October presents to one of my preferred occasions - Halloween. It's a fabulous opportunity to get together and disclose to one another creepy stories and peculiar happenings. It's additionally incredible for the children because of the measure of sweets they get stunt or treating! Anyway, for a few of us who will be working and voyaging, sadly, we won't have the option to test the pleasures of Halloween or, on the other hand, will we?

In the event that you are traversing the UK this month, you better look out for frightens on your movements - even the air terminals aren't protected from the things that go knock in the night. We examine one of the UK's most haunted air terminals.

Heathrow is one of the busiest UK air terminals and handles the most noteworthy number of global explorers in the world. It is astonishing to find that Heathrow is likewise the most haunted air terminal in the UK and one that is haunted by conceivably the most popular bandit in Britain - Dick Turpin.

Dick Turpin was loved by the poor as he ransacked from the rich to fill his pockets anyway. It is the endeavors of his group that got him the greatest press inclusion some time ago. Endeavors of his pack included homicide, setting individuals ablaze (while alive) and torment. At the point when at last contracted, he was condemned to the terrible bug by hangman's tree - evidently with a grin all over. So how does this identify with Heathrow? Dick Turpin being a roadway man, implies that he is continually moving to start with one open door then onto the next - even in the afterlife.

Sightings of Turpin have been accounted for along the A1 motorway and specifically Heathrow Airport. A portion of the individuals who work at Heathrow expresses that they can feel the hot breath on the rear of their necks, followed by the calls of a man woofing.

Another well-known episode follows the heartbreaking accident of a Belgian Airlines Plane in 1948. The carrier crash was a consequence of a bombed arriving during a hefty haze and accepted the lives of every body. Notwithstanding this, the crisis administrations attempted to battle through the plane destruction to see whether there were any survivors. As the men worked through, they were drawn nearer by a man in a cap who asked whether they had discovered his attaché. Surprised, the men went to see the man blur away into the haze. Later they found the body of the man profound inside the destruction. The man, wearing dark, is accounted for to frequent the VIP parlor of Heathrow and the busiest pieces of the runway actually searching for his attaché. A few voyagers even report sightings of dim legs without any bodies sitting at desolate seats.

So, there you go - from acclaimed apparitions to sadly misfortunes, it appears to be that Heathrow is significantly busier than you most likely think. Recollect whether you feel a consuming warmth or the sound of frantic canines when you are separated from everyone else in Heathrow. Don't think back - you probably won't care for what you see.

Explorers staying in London on an excursion for the brief-term work want to remain in London lodgings close to the air terminal. There is a wide scope of London Heathrow lodgings having phenomenal rates. There are modest lodgings close to the air terminal just as top quality inns close to the air terminal. The individuals who need to get an early flight have the choice of remaining in a lodging close to the air terminal. Numerous explorers visiting London for a brief timeframe need to get a trip inside hours, so they have the handy issue of remaining for a night at some lodging. The London inns close to the air terminal offer stopping bundles and furthermore housing to the visitors.

Regardless of whether you are on a work excursion or on a delay for a corresponding flight, there are London inns going from two-star inns, modest air terminal inns to better quality extravagance air terminal inns.

Chiswick Moran Hotel is situated in a tree-lined Chiswick High Road. Its area is extraordinary as it has equivalent separation to Central London. It has excellent vehicle connect. Besides, it is an upscale lodging housed in green environmental factors.

Another inn in London close to the air terminal is the Comfort Hotel. It is arranged close to the air terminal and furthermore to the Stockley Park. There is authentic air terminal transport administration from the air terminal to the inn. A considerable lot of the vacation destinations like Windsor, Eton and Lego land amusement park are found close by. This inn's rooms are agreeable, and not many of the exclusive rooms have cooling in them.

An advantageous London Hotel for the business voyager is the Park Inn lodging. It is exceptionally close to the air terminal and is very appropriate for the business voyagers, gathering representatives and recreation visitors. It is a lavish lodging, having a pool and Jacuzzi. There is transport administration from the air terminal. There is also a live air terminal association on TV where the deferral of appearance and flight is shown. As it is a four-star lodging, it has all the standard luxuries in the room.

The Holiday Inn Hotel in Heathrow London inn isn't just a couple of moments from the air terminal yet near the focal London. It is situated close to Stockley Business Park and Bed Font Lakes. The rooms are cooled, extensive and appropriate for family. It is all around situated for gatherings and meetings at Heathrow. The vehicle leaving the office is given to the visitors.

The Crowne Plaza Hotel London is another inn arranged close to the air terminal. It is situated close to the primary throughways M4 and M40. Vacation spots like Earl's Court, Olympia and Stockley Park are altogether exceptionally close to it. Focal London attractions like Lego land, Windsor, Ascot Racecourse, Wembley and Twickenham are effectively agreeable. The rooms are enormous and have present-day offices.

It has a nine opening green as well. So ,if your flight is postponed, you can have a series of golf to unwind at that point.

The Holiday Inn London Ariel is arranged exceptionally near the Heathrow air terminal. The lodgings are planned with power outage rooms having twofold coated windows to help with a decent night's rest. The stopping of the lodging is at a sensible rate, including a meeting community for the business explorer. The rooms have cooling just as rapid web association.

By the same Collection:

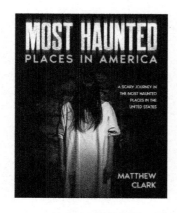

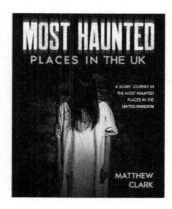

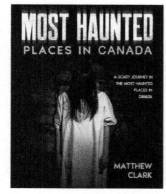

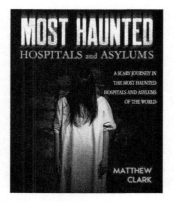

Search on Amazon!!

Printed in Great Britain
by Amazon

84648077R00059